THE TOMB OF ꜣIP
AT EL SAFF

Papyrus thicket, with birds, at center of right wall of the tomb of *Ip* at El Saff

THE TOMB OF *'IP* AT EL SAFF

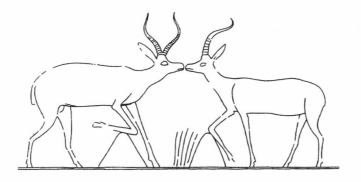

by Henry George Fischer

Curator Emeritus, Egyptian Art,
The Metropolitan Museum of Art

The Metropolitan Museum of Art
New York 1996

Title page: Two gazelles face each other in the
hunting scene on the right wall of the tomb of Ip

Typeset in New Baskerville
Designed by Henry G. Fischer and Peter Der Manuelian
Typeset and produced by Peter Der Manuelian, Boston, Massachusetts

ISBN 0-87099-756-4

Printed and manufactured in the United States of America by
The Stinehour Press, Lunenburg, Vermont

To the memory of
Labib Habachi
(1906–1984)

Contents

Preface

BEFORE PRESENTING THE MATERIAL that is offered in this monograph, I should like to pay a few words of tribute, as one of the very many to whom Labib Habachi extended the warmth of his friendship and the wealth of his knowledge concerning the archaeological sites throughout Egypt. I hope, above all, to correct any impression I may give, in the following pages, that he was unwilling to share information with his colleagues. Indeed it was precisely because he was so generous that I did not, on occasion, wish to press him for more. I had his help from the moment I first met him, in 1955, when he personally took me to the Old Kingdom cemetery of Gozeriya and enabled me to record the inscriptions that had been found there (as noted subsequently in my *Dendera*, p. viii). In the following year he enabled me to visit Moʿalla (*WZKM* 57 [1961], 59), and he later gave me the possibility of publishing some early inscriptions from Busiris (*MMJ* 11 [1976], 157). That is not all, but it gives some idea of my indebtedness to him.

As for the worth of his contribution to Egyptology, I can do no better than to quote the words of George Hughes, when he joined Jaroslav Černý and Wolfgang Helck in warmly endorsing Labib's honorary doctorate from New York University in 1966:

> It would be difficult to recount his many abilities and accomplishments, but I have often said in recent years that there is probably no one living today who knows so much about the antiquities of ancient Egypt first hand, not simply where they are but what they mean. . . . In a long career in the Department of Antiquities, from the lowest rank to Chief Inspector, he was stationed at most posts throughout Egypt at one time or another, and his background and instincts caused him to see the monuments in his charge wherever he was, not through the eyes of the civil servant, but of the scholar. In addition, he has an amazing knowledge of the Egyptian collections in the world's great museums.
>
> There has come a long series of articles and monographs from his pen, nearly every one of them producing some hitherto unknown material and a new interpretation of known material. He has been the scholarly head of

numerous major excavations in Egypt, and resulting volumes of basic importance by him have appeared or are awaiting publication. He is never satisfied
with a mere excavation report of finds but gives them a thoroughgoing
interpretation.

To which I shall add only a few words from Helck's strikingly similar testi-
mony: "Sein Spürsinn läßt ihn auch dort, wo andere schon vor ihm geforscht
haben, Neues und oft Entscheidenes entdecken. . . . Immer bringen die
Veröffentlichungen von Herrn Labib etwas Neues, oft etwas Überraschendes."

List of Figures

List of Plates

1. The documentation

DURING A VISIT THAT LABIB HABACHI made to my home in Sherman, Connecticut, in 1973, I showed him a series of photographs I had purchased at the Cairo Museum many years earlier, and which bore no identification. After a moment of surprise, he told me that they belonged to a tomb at El Saff, near Atfih, which was cleared in 1936; but he seemed reluctant to say more, and I judged, from his reticence, that this was something he himself intended to publish. Indeed it was probably one of his earliest projects, for he became Inspector in the Department of Antiquities in 1930 and his earliest publication, in 1937, concerned a site in the Fayum.[1] The tomb thus came within the district he was supervising at the time, and he was probably personally responsible for its clearance.[2]

I felt that I should not press Labib for further information and he did not mention the matter again. In 1988, however, four years after his death, I sent an inquiry to Chicago House, in Luxor, to find out if he had made further progress with his project; by that time all his papers had been assembled there and were being sorted out by Henry Riad. Thanks to him, and to Lanny Bell, who was then director, I learned that, although no trace could be found of a manuscript or notes, or any map or plan, there were a number of inked tracings of the scenes and inscriptions, as well as four watercolor paintings showing details, and some photographs.

---

[1] "Une 'vaste salle' d'Amenemhat III à Kiman-Farès (Fayoum)," *ASAE* 37 (1937), 85–95.

[2] Werner Kaiser, *MDAIK* 17 (1961), 41, cites Junker's report that the Egyptian Department of Antiquities excavated a predynastic cemetery in the 1930's (*Abhandlungen der Preußischen Akademie der Wissenschaften, phil.-hist. Klasse,* 1941, Nr. 6, p. 54). He attempted to relocate this site and found two concentrations of burials northeast of the town ("im Nordostteil von El-Saff"). In a later article, "Ein Friedhof der Maadi-kultur bei es-Saff," (*MDAIK* 41 [1985], 43–46), he offers further information, based on records that Labib Habachi made in the course of these excavations, towards the end of 1935. The records include a cadastral map on which the burials were inserted; they are situated at a point about 1 km north of the village, just east of Ezba El Markaz. But, as Kaiser has assured me, there is no indication of any tomb such as that of *Ip*, and all the burials that were recorded are predynastic.

All of this material was kindly entrusted to me for publication. When it arrived, I found, to my surprise, that the photographs included only a few uninteresting details, reduplicating parts of what I already had in hand, as well as some details of scenes that were completely unknown to me, and which I took to belong to a burial chamber. These new scenes also appeared in two of the four watercolor paintings. The tracings, on the other hand, all concerned the chapel that appeared in my photographs, and were very nearly complete. Their relative position in the chapel could be seen from a close examination of the photograph of the rear wall shown in Pl. 5. And finally, by measuring the drawings, it was possible to estimate the dimensions of the chamber, which proved to be about three metres long and about half that much in breadth. The only remaining problem, so far as their assemblage is concerned, was the precise position of a scene showing the owner shaking papyrus stalks in the marshes (Pl. E), although there could be little doubt about its approximate location.

A more difficult problem, of a different kind, was presented by the state of some of the drawings. Although half of them are on very old tracing paper, which has become brittle and yellow, with considerable darkening, they could still be used in their present state. But the other five, on newer paper, required further attention despite their freshness. They were evidently retraced from the originals, which were then discarded, and while the penciled retracing seems to have been done with care, it was then inked less skillfully, so that the lines in ink and pencil do not always match. After some discussion with Peter Dorman, the present director at Chicago House, it was decided that these drawings should be left as they are, and that they would have to be completely redrawn, following the penciled line wherever there was any deviation. The revised copies have been executed most satisfactorily by Peter Der Manuelian, incorporating a few small corrections that I was able to make by comparing the photograph on Pls. 3c and 4. To these I have myself added a small drawing, made to scale from the photograph on Pl. 3b, which supplies four short columns of inscription that had been overlooked when the copies were made in 1936.[3]

---

[3] The original drawings and paintings are again at Chicago House, and the photographs in my possession, along with the new tracings, are to be placed in the Egyptian Department of The Metropolitan Museum after publication.

On the whole, the original copies are excellent, but those who made them were up against considerable difficulties, for the decoration is solely painted, without any underlying relief, and many areas were only faintly visible or were altogether erased. Some improvements could doubtless be made by re–examining the tomb itself, and Dieter Arnold, who has been working at Lisht, has helpfully attempted to relocate it, without success. Even if it were rediscovered, however, it seems unlikely that the paintings would be as well preserved as they were when they were first uncovered, and the present documentation therefore seems well worth publishing in its present state.

In the following listing of the epigraphic record, the tracings that have been redrawn or added are presented in italic type:

1. LEFT WALL: *Seated couple, at left end, receive offerings* (Pl. B).

2. *Continuation rightward of text above them, and offering list* (Pls. B, C).

3. *Further continuation rightward of offering list, and short registers* (Pl. C).

4. RIGHT WALL: Hunting scene at left end, with pair of gazelles (Pl. D; also in color, Pl. 6).

5. Dog at right end of this scene (Pl. D).

6. Registers below this scene, with half-effaced figures (Pl. D).

7. *Couple in bark, at lower right of same scene, owner shaking papyrus* (Pl. E).

7a. *Inscription above this (completed from photograph, Pl. 3b)* (Pl. E).

8. Papyrus thicket, with birds, at center of wall (Pl. E, also in color, Frontispiece).

9. *Couple in bark, at right, owner spearing fish* (Pl. F).

10. REAR WALL: Owner at right, viewing cattle (Pl. G).

11. Recording and presentation of cattle at left (Pl. G).

The drawings, throughout Plates B–G, have been reduced to a scale of 1:5. To these must be added the two watercolor copies showing parts of the presumed burial chamber (Pl. 7).

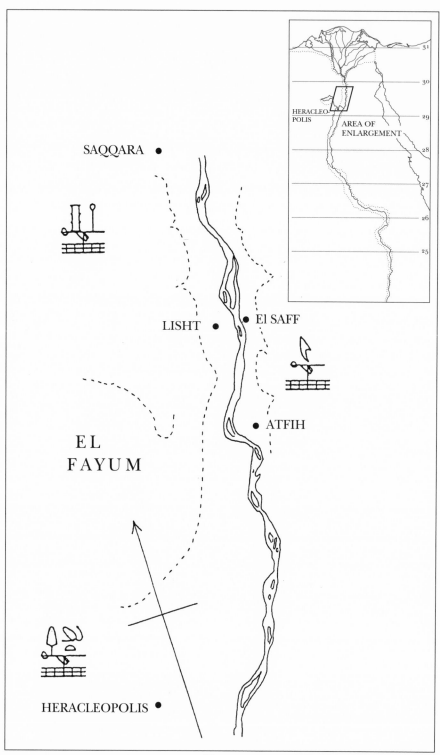

Fig. 1

2. The orientation of the tomb

As noted earlier, El Saff is situated near Atfih, and like Atfih, which lies about 17 km to the south of it, it is on the east side of the river (Fig. 1). The tomb of *Ip* was presumably cut into the desert escarpment behind the town, and the resultant reversal of the more usual orientation is doubtless responsible for the apparent absence of an offering place or false door. As may be seen from the Sixth Dynasty rock tombs at Sheikh Said, an effort was often made, in such cases, to locate the offering niche on a west wall. In two of the earliest Middle Kingdom tombs at Beni Hasan, which were similarly located on the east side, the offering place is again at the west end, south of the entrance.[4] In the present case, since the width of the tomb was no more than half its length, i.e., about 150 cm, there would hardly have been room for it in that location unless the entrance were not centered, but placed well to one side. Assuming that the orientation was much the same as in these tombs at Beni Hasan, it is remarkable that the offering list is at the east end of the north (left) wall, whereas at Beni Hasan, regardless of whether the offering place is at the east or west end, the list is located at the southeast corner.[5] From this it seems likely that *Ip*'s offering place was at the northwest corner of his chapel, behind the seated couple toward whom the offering list is directed. The corner may be seen in Pl. 1, including about 12 cm of the adjacent wall, but it is not possible to say whether or not this wall was painted.

This may be the most opportune place to note that the right-hand (presumably southern) wall has been opened along the top for a length of almost 90 cm, as observed from the photographs shown in Pl. 3a–b. The opening is evidently ancient, for the surface beneath it is eroded. Leafy branches are visible along the aperture, perhaps placed there by the excavators to effect a

---

[4] Most conveniently seen in the Porter-Moss *Topographical Bibliography*, Vol. IV (Oxford 1934), p. 150: tomb 17 (24); tomb 33 (9).

[5] *Ibid.*, tomb 17 (14): tomb 33 (6). At offering place, or adjacent to it: tomb 15 (23); tomb 29 (10).

temporary blockage. Quite possibly it was this aperture that led to the discovery of the chapel.

Although it is highly probable that the longitudinal axis of the chapel was indeed oriented west–east, I have considered it safer, in the absence of any record of the chapel's precise location, to refer to the three walls that have been recorded as "right," "left," and "rear" or "back," as in the previous listing; they will, on occasion, be abbreviated as "R," "L," and "B."

Discussions of the titles and of the date will be left until later (Chapters 4 and 5), since they make use of restorations that are dealt with in the following pages.

3.1 The left wall (Pls. 1–2, B–C)

AT THE LEFT END, facing inward toward the rear of the chapel, the deceased owner and his wife are shown seated upon a lion-legged chair,[6] the grain of its wood indicated by undulating stripes.[7] It is not clear whether there was any support for the back. The owner has a shoulder-length wig and short beard. He wears a short, tight-fitting kilt, a broad collar and at least one bracelet. One hand is stretched out to receive offerings, while the other raises a jar of unguent to his nose.[8] His wife has a long lappeted wig, adorned with a fillet, which, from a close examination of the photograph, appears to have the customary streamers. She wears a long close-fitting dress, which probably had shoulder straps although no trace of them is visible, and similarly has a broad collar. She embraces her husband in conventional manner, with one hand placed on an arm, and the other clasping the shoulder farthest from her. Nothing in this scene is any different from what was usual in the late Old Kingdom and the Heracleopolitan Period, with the possible exception of the lappeted wig, which was coming back in vogue, after having been, for some time, more frequently replaced by a shorter one.[9]

In front of the couple is the offering of a goose, which was probably held by a standing figure, and beyond him, in a low register that extends down the length of the wall, is a procession of smaller offering-bearers, of whom only a single man and woman survive. The couple are identified in a series of 16 columns of inscription above them, which also contain a number of rather conventional autobiographical statements. Most of the remaining space beyond this is occupied by an offering list containing 54 compartments. Two lines of inscription are placed above the list, one apparently continuing the

---

[6] As seen from a photograph not shown here.

[7] Less stylized in Old Kingdom examples: e.g., Blackman, *Meir* IV, pls. 14–15. But sinuous lines are again to be seen in the early Middle Kingdom: Davies, *Antefoḳer*, pl. 25.

[8] This motif was introduced in the Sixth Dynasty; see Nadine Cherpion, *Mastabas*, pp. 54, 178. Its later use is discussed below, at the end of Chapter 5.

[9] Cf. my *Egyptian Studies* III, chap. 3, n. 17.

autobiographical statements, but much damaged, and the second containing an offering formula. To the right of the offering list are three short registers, the uppermost of which shows male offering bearers and some of their offerings, including a jar (perhaps suspended from a bar across the shoulders of the man in front) and two pairs of sandals. The bottom register contains a group of three men in a papyrus skiff, one of them steering or paddling with a long oar, while the two others haul in a seining net full of fish, among which a bolti and two mullets are identifiable.[10]

The main inscription is retrograde, reading from left to right:[11] (1) His wife, his [beloved], *Mnḫt Ḥnwt*,[a] (2) She Who is Known to the King, revered with Hathor, the Mistress of Atfih.[b] (3) He who is [revered] with Anubis, Sole Companion, Keeper of the Diadem, (4) Overseer[c] of the Western Desert, Overseer of Marshlands, (5) Overseer of the Cattle Estate, Overseer of Vegetation, (6) Over[seer] of.... Overseer of the Two Fields of Offerings, (7) Over[seer] of..., Overseer of the Army, *Ip*.[d] (8) "I exercised [thi]s [office][e] under the majesty of my lord when [I] (9) [was in the serv]ice of his majesty,[f] one who was noble and efficient every day with his [majesty], (10) [more than] any dignitary[g] of his, my heart being[h] stalwart for his majesty (11) concerning all that I did. I came from my town and went down (12) in my cemetery[i] having done what the king praises (13) and his officials order[j] in excellence and efficacy[k] because the king ordered[l] me, and [nothing] came amiss (14) in me.[m] And having built a house, dug a canal, excavated a pool, and planted (15) sycamore trees.[n] And dispelled misery from him who sustained affliction,[o] by my character(?)[p] (16) and by what I did. I made this work of the necropolis(?),[q] of the place of reverence with the king, with Osi[ris], and [with(?)] my children(?)" (17)[r] .... (18)[s] An offering that the king gives, and Osiris, Lord of Busiris, [the Great God, Lord of Aby]dos, that offerings be invoked in his tomb that is in the western desert, [the Chancellor of the King of Lower Egypt], the Sole [Companion], the *Smꜣ*-Priest, the revered *Ipi*.

---

[10] For this scene see Oric Bates in *Harvard African Studies* 1 (1917), 258–63; Douglas Brewer and Renée Friedman, *Fish and Fishing in Ancient Egypt* (Warminster 1989), pp. 42–46; Harpur, *Decoration*, pp. 145–49.

[11] This may be explained by the fact that the inscription contains a statement. For the use of retrograde sequence in such cases, which has its beginnings in the Sixth Dynasty, see my *Egyptian Studies* II, p. 56, and *L'écriture,* pp. 111, 124.

COMMENTS:

(a) To be restored as shown in Fig. 2. The double name is to be added to those collected by Pascal Vernus, *Le Surnom au Moyen Empire* (Paris 1986). For *Mnḫt* see *PN* I, 153 (14), and cf. *ibid.*, (15, 16) as well as (3) masculine *Mnḫ*, all known from the Middle Kingdom, and not earlier. For *Ḥnwt* see *PN* I, 242 (18) and cf. *ibid.*, (14, 17), as well as n. 43 below.

Fig. 2

(b) The photograph shows traces of the plural sign (three pellets) that should follow *Tp-iḥw*. For Middle Kingdom references to this place, now Atfih, see Gomaà, *Besiedlung* I, pp. 380–81. The example he cites from H. Lutz, *Egyptian Tomb Steles*, pl. 9, is apparently earlier than the end of the Old Kingdom, as is another, on the obelisk shown in Jéquier, *Monument funéraire de Pepi II*, III (Cairo 1940), fig. 57, where it follows the name *Idw*. This is probably a second personal name, although only one other example of such a name is known, and it is applied to a woman of the New Kingdom (*PN* I, 380 [1]). But it possibly refers to the locality to which the owner belonged, as on some Old Kingdom obelisks mentioning Heliopolis (BM 495, Cairo CG 17001, 17002); in these cases, however, the place is mentioned in connection with the titles, and does not follow the name.

(c) For the interpretation see Chapter 4 below, title 3.

(d) For this very common Middle Kingdom name see *PN* I, 21 (29). In this tomb, as sometimes elsewhere, it interchanges with ⸢⸣ *PN* I, 22 [15]), which is also common in the Old Kingdom. The addition of the final ⸢⸣ cannot be equated with the determinative ⸢⸣ (discussed in my *Coptite Nome*, pp. 124–25), since it occurs in proximity to the figure of the owner.

(e) Restoring ⸢⸣, referring to the title "overseer of the army," which has just been mentioned before *Ipi*'s name.

(f) Restoring ⸢⸣ at the bottom of the preceding column, and then ⸢⸣. For other references to serving the king (*šms nswt*), all from Dyns. XI–XII, see Janssen, *Trad. Autobiogr.* I, pp. 111–12. As his first examples show, this use of *šms* was already attested in the Heracleopolitan Period; cf. also *WZKM* 57 (1961), 69–71.

(g) Restoring ⸢⸣ at the bottom of the preceding column, and then

[⌐]〗. The available space clearly indicates the Middle Kingdom writing *siḥ* rather than *sʿḥ*. Cf. *špss ḥr ḥm n nb(.i) r sʿḥ[.f nb]* (*Urk.* I, 119 [12]), from the reign of Pepy II; see Janssen, *Trad. Autobiogr.*, pp. 33–34, where it may be seen that all such phrases likewise belong to the Old Kingdom. Another Old Kingdom passage of this kind combines *špss* and *mnḫ* as is done here: *Urk.* I, 60 (7).

(h) The word *sk* is evidently to be read here, although there is no trace of the handle of ⌐, and it may not have been added, for the sign is centered; perhaps this is a scribal error. The phrase *sk nḫt ib(.i) n ḥm.f* is known twice from Dyn. VI: *Urk.* I, 85 (14), 195 (5). And it continues very similarly in both cases.

(i) Restoring [〰] at the bottom of col. 11. This phrase, which occurs at the head of the Old Kingdom traditional autobiography, is displaced in this instance because the foregoing phrases continue the allusion to the owner's title that precedes his name. For other examples see Edel, *MDAIK* 13 (1944), 47–48, and Janssen, *Trad. Autobiogr.*, 38–39, 83–84. Eric Doret, *The Narrative Verbal System of Old and Middle Egyptian* (Geneva 1986), pp. 152–53, provides grounds for accepting the interpretation of *spȝt* as "necropolis," as proposed by Goedicke, *Orientalia* 24 (1955), 225–39, which I have previously doubted.

(j) This recalls an epithet that occurs in the inscriptions of two late Old Kingdom nomarchs at Dendera: *rs-tp r wḏt srw* "vigilant concerning what the officials order," the *srw* being agents of the king (Fischer, *Dendera*, pp. 100–101, 114).

(k) *Wb.* II, 85 (22), has no example of *bw mnḫ* before Dyn. XXII, but it is known from Dyn VI: *Urk.* I, 205 (6, 14), and T.G.H. James and M.R. Apted, *Mastaba of Khentika* (London 1953), pl. 39 (217). For *bw iqr* (*Wb.* I, 137 [10]) the earliest example cited is from the reign of Sesostris I (Siut I, 249). Other compounds of this kind are well known from the Old Kingdom; Edel, *Altäg. Gramm.*, §261, mentions *bw nfr* and *bw mȝʿ*, to which may also be added *bw ʿȝ* "much" (*Urk.* I, 222 [1]). The omission of *r* in *iqr* is known from the reign of Sesostris III: J. Couyat and P. Montet, *Inscriptions… du Ouadi Hammamat* (Cairo 1912), no. 47 (8, 12); but it also occurs as early as the Heracleopolitan Period in the name of the god *Iq(r)*: Fischer, *Dendera*, pp. 13, 208.

(l) The tall sign copied as ⌐ actually looks more like ⌐ on the photograph, and despite the odd arrangement of signs, I see no other solution than *n wḏ*

n(.i) nswt. Note that *nswt* is 𓊹𓈖, as in the preceding column; unlike title 13 in Chapter 4.

(m) Restoring 𓂋𓏥𓀀𓅯𓏏𓂋 at the end of col. 13. The translation follows Clère's interpretation in *Ägyptologische Studien* (Berlin 1955), 38–43.

(n) This essentially follows the Old Kingdom formula discussed by Edel, *MDAIK* 13 (1944), 49–50. For the Middle Kingdom see Newberry, *Bersheh* II, pl. 21 (left wall, 12–13), and CT II, 134; III, 94; VI, 171; VII, 209, 239. The last of these is similar in that it mentions digging both a pool and a canal. The verb *šꜣd* is used in nearly all these cases, but it is likewise applied to the digging of a canal, as here, in *Urk.* I, 220 (15–16). For the verb and subject of *šdi.n(.i) šdw,* both derived from *šdi* in the sense of "remove," see Faulkner, *Concise Dictionary* (Oxford 1962), pp. 273–74. *Wdi* also occurs in CT VI, 171, thus supplying another Middle Kingdom example of this use of the verb in the sense of "plant." The signs 𓈖𓈖 must be restored at the bottom of col. 14 for *wdi[.n](.i)* and [*n*]*hwt.*

(o) Old Kingdom parallels are to be found in *Urk.* I, 269 (6), 271 (8), although these have *sꜣry* rather than *ḥry sꜣr.* See also Edel, *ZÄS* 81 (1956), 8, who discusses *iw.* The final sign evidently represents 𓃂.

(p) The critical sign does not look exactly like *qd* in the preceding column, but I can make no better suggestion.

(q) Assuming that the sign may be 𓏤 rather than 𓏥.

(r) This line probably continues the preceding columns, and appears to be retrograde. If so, an interpretation of the remaining signs is doubly difficult, because retrograde sequence within a single line often recurrently reverts to the normal order of the signs within the individual words; cf. Fischer, *L'écriture,* p. 115 and fig. 43. The initial words seem to be *snwt(.i) mr(.i) ḏt(.i) mr(.i)* "my beloved siblings, my beloved servants," but, except for isolated words, the rest is difficult to follow.

(s) See Figure 3 for the restorations in this line, which is not retrograde, and in which the signs address the deceased, conforming to the orientation of the list of offerings below them.

Very few of the entries in the offering list are legible except for those in the first four compartments: (1) Pouring water, burning [incense]. (2) Libation

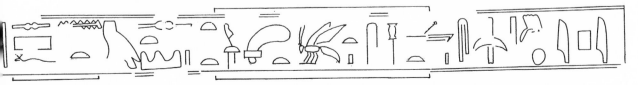

Fig. 3

(of natron) 2 pellets. (3) Pellet of natron (*bd*). (4) Pellet of incense (*snṯr*). Further traces have been detected after long scrutiny of a photograph (not illustrated) that shows compartments 9–16, and the most certain of these traces are shown in Fig. 4. Compartments 12–13 evidently begin with *mnw ḥḏ* and *mnw km* "white and black *mnw*-stone," for which see Hassan, *Gîza* VI/2, pp. 193–94. Compartment 14 lists the first three of the traditional series of seven ointments: *stỉ ḥb, ḥknw, sfṯ;* the rest presumably followed in compartments 15 and 16, and the latter probably has [*ḥȝtt*] *ṯ[ḥnw]*. The group ∤ ◁ in (9) is puzzling, for this compartment seems to refer to *ḥḏ mnw* and *km mnw*, as in (12–13); possibly the reed leaf belongs to *ỉ[rp]*; cf. *ibid.*, pp. 198–99. In (10) the trace above ⸨ looks like the handle of ◇ (oriented as in compartment 14), suggesting *psšḳf* (*ibid.*, pp. 186–87), but the space above it would then be hard to explain. The identification of these and other traces is difficult because the compartments contain more than a single entry, and because the sequence of the entries is somewhat unusual.

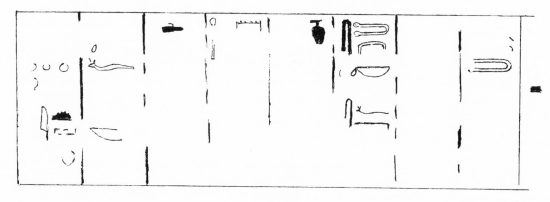

Fig. 4

3.2 The right wall (Pls. 3–4, 6, D–E, Frontispiece)

THE DOMINANT FEATURES OF THIS WALL are two groups showing the owner standing in a papyrus bark, accompanied by the seated figure of his wife, with each group facing inward. In the scene on the left he brandishes a stalk of papyrus in one hand and grasps a standing stalk with the other. This is the traditional rite elsewhere identified as *zšš wꜣḏ n Ḥtḥr* "rattling papyrus for Hathor."[12] The attire of the owner is remarkable, for he not only wears a short wig and dressy kilt with projecting front,[13] but also the distinctive bandoleer of a lector priest,[14] which seems, quite exceptionally, to emphasize the religious aspect of this activity.[15] His wife, wearing a long dress, long lappeted wig and bracelet, crooks an arm around one leg of her husband. In the corresponding scene on the right, where the owner is spearing fish, he has short hair and is dressed much more simply in a short, tight-fitting kilt. In this case the figure of the wife is separate, and only her head is visible, again wearing a long lappeted wig. She is labeled "his wife, his beloved," but her name is lost. A small male figure stands behind the owner at a level well above the boat, with two fishes hanging from an extended hand. He too is labeled, but nothing of this remains but the sign for *r*.

Between the two boating scenes is a papyus thicket, above which are a number of birds. Two kingfishers in flight are to be found at the upper and lower right of the group, displaying—for the first time—all the colorful plumage of

---

[12] Principally known from the Old Kingdom. For the evidence see Harpur, *Decoration*, pp. 335–38, and *GM* 38 (1980), 53–61, where the motif is discussed in detail. It reappears, at the beginning of the Middle Kingdom, in Newberry, *Beni Hasan* II, pl. 4. Montet, *Kêmi* 14 (1957), 104, notes that it also occurs in an archaizing relief of Dyn. XXVI: Maspero, *Le Musée Egyptien* 2 (Cairo 1907), 31 and pl. 35. Harpur's emphasis on the ritualistic nature of this is sound, but I still prefer Balcz's translation of *zšš* (*ZÄS* 75 [1939], 36) as "Schütteln" rather than "pulling."

[13] Harpur, *loc. cit.*, observes that the same type of kilt is worn in many other examples of this scene.

[14] For this attire see E. Staehelin, *Untersuchungen zur ägyptischen Tracht im Alten Reich* (Berlin 1966), pp. 80–84. She notes that it is sometimes worn by officials who are not known to have the title of lector priest, and that the shorter style of wig is sometimes worn when the priest is not actually officiating.

[15] Which might bear out the conclusions of Yvonne Harpur's article, cited in n. 12 above.

the halcyons.[16] The birds flying between them appear to be a shrike and pigeon. An egret is perched on a stalk of papyrus, and the bird rising from the thicket may be a pintailed duck, although the form of the tail is very strange. The remaining birds are various kinds of ducks and geese.

A series of five registers occupies the left end of the wall, of which only the uppermost is at all well preserved. This is a hunting scene, featuring two gazelles, probably a male and female, each raising a foreleg against a reddish mound,[17] and facing each other symmetrically, nose-to-nose;[18] they may represent two slightly different species—*gḥs* and *gsꜣ*.[19] The one at the left is attacked from the rear by a hunting dog. Above the other is a hedgehog within a semicircular hoop that seems to have cord wound around it (Fig. 5), and evidently represents a trap; although I know of no other example of such traps for small mammals, it seems likely enough that they were used.[20] At the right end of the register a standing man raises one hand in the direction of a second dog, but the context is lost. The taller register below this one shows the head and other traces of two men walking rightward; the one at the left may be carrying a small animal, and perhaps both are returning from the chase. Little may be made of the figures in the three smaller registers at the bottom.

Fig. 5

---

[16] Other representations of this species (*alcedo atthis*) are cited by Harpur, *Decoration*, p. 185, n. 134; see also Patrick F. Houlihan, *Birds of Ancient Egypt* (Warminster 1986), pp. 113–14, a work I have consulted for other identifications, although its usefulness for that purpose is rather limited.

[17] For the attitude, with one leg resting on a rise in the desert, cf. Paget and Pirie, *Tomb of Ptah-hetep*, pl. 32; also, dating to the early Twelfth Dynasty, Davies, *Antefoker*, frontispiece and pl. 6.

[18] For symmetry in Old Kingdom reliefs see the several examples collected by Balcz, *MDAIK* 1 (1930), 137–52. In some cases, such as his fig. 2, this is to be attributed to provincial ineptness; so also the unusual degree of symmetry that is to be seen in Kanawati, *Hawawish* I, pls. 8, 10, 11, 15, which seems to be later than the Old Kingdom (cf. Brovarski, *BdE* 97/1 [1985], 134); for an Eleventh Dynasty example, very comparable to the present one, see C. Vandersleyen, *Das Alte Ägypten: Propyläen Kunstgeschichte* 15 (Berlin 1975), pl. 262.

[19] Cf. Wild, *Ti* III, pl. 166; the tail of *gsꜣ* is longer in R. Macramallah, *Mastaba d'Idout* (Cairo 1935), pl. 20; there (p. 41) it is identified as *Gazella Isabella*, Gray. The same pair of gazelles are shown side by side in L. Borchardt, *Grabdenkmal des Königs SaꜣḥureꜤ* II (Leipzig 1913), pl. 17.

[20] A kid oddly appears in an enclosure of similar appearance in Hassan, *Saqqara* I, fig. 12. There can hardly be any question, however, that hedgehogs were trapped, for they are often shown alive in cages in tomb chapels of the Old Kingdom: see Vera von Droste zu Hülshoff, *Der Igel im alten Ägypten* (Hildesheim 1980), figs. 26–33; a Twelfth Dynasty example in fig. 34.

At the opposite end of the wall, beyond an inscription belonging to the fishing scene, there is a very small register containing a single female offering bearer. She has a long lappeted wig and long dress, and carries a basket on her head, supporting it with one hand. Her name appears in a small inscription in front of her: *Ktt.*[21]

The two principal inscriptions, above the boating scenes, are again retrograde,[22] the signs facing inward, towards the center of the wall, and reading inwards. On the left side: (1) One revered with Osiris, [*Ip*] (2) One Who is Known to the King, *I[p]*, (3) one who truly fills the heart of the king (with confidence), *Ip[i]*, (4) Chancellor of the King of Lower Egypt, the revered *Ip*, (5) the Sole Companion, Overseer of ___, *Ip*. On the right side: (6) One revered with Anubis (7) Who is Upon His Mountain ... (8) ... Anubis ...[a] (9) ... (10) [Overseer] of the Storehouse of Tenant Landholders [of the Great House], Companion of the House, (11) Inspector of Tenant Landownwers [of the Great House], (12) Functionary of Tenant Landholding of the Great House, (13) Overseer of Upper Egyptian Nomes 20–21, Judge of That Which One Alone Judges, who does that which his lord[b] praises, (14) who is loved by him. Spearing many fish.[c]

COMMENTS:

(a) I have no explanation for this apparent reappearance of Anubis.

(b) Emending to 𝕛 ⚌ ☐. This area cannot be seen in the photograph, being covered with an accretion; the sign ⌣, may be a scribal error. For the form of 𝕛, known as early as the Old Kingdom, see my *Egyptian Studies* III, chap. 14, section 13.

(c) Note the traditional use of graphic dissimilation; the three species of fish are Tilapia (Sign List K1), mullet (K3) and Barbus bynni (K2). Since *ʿšt* is feminine, the term for fish must be *mḥyt*.

[21] Occurs on a late Middle Kingdom stela: Janine Monnet Saleh, *Antiquités égyptiennes de Zagreb* (Paris 1970), no. 8. Cf. ⌣ (*PN* I, 349 [15] and ⌣ ° [27]), also Middle Kingdom.

[22] Presumably this simply continues the more logical use of it on the left wall. The sequence of R1–5 is evident from the order of titles in the last two columns.

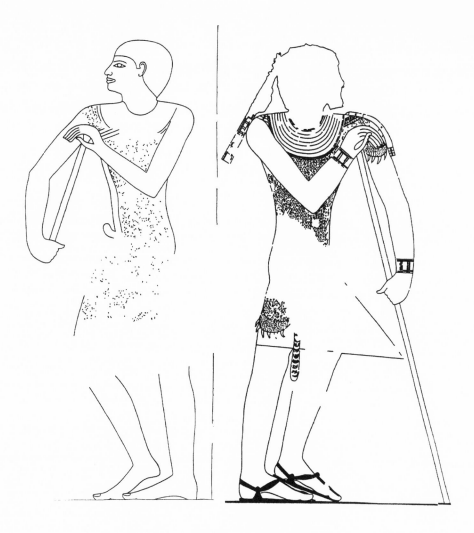

Fig. 6

3.3 The rear wall (Pls. 5, G)

THE TOP OF THE PAINTED AREA is at the same level as that of the walls on either side, but is about 30 percent shorter. At the right, facing left, is a large-scale figure of the owner, who assumes an attitude that is well known from the Old Kingdom; he stands leaning against his staff, with one knee flexed so that the heel is off the ground.[23] He has short hair and is beardless. A leopard-skin mantle[24] all but covers his kilt, of which scarcely anything is to be seen but the projecting tab of the belt. He also wears a broad collar, which apparently overlaps the mantle, but it seems doubtful that the mantle covered the forward shoulder, as it usually does, since a series of diagonal lines beyond the raised hand evidently demarcates its upper border, running to the shoulder opposite. Although the leopard skin, well known from earlier times, continued to be applied to the tomb owner at the beginning of the Middle Kingdom,[25] it was thereafter reserved for its long-established use as a priestly adornment.[26]

Among the parallels for *Ip*'s attitude and attire from the Old Kingdom, the one shown in Fig. 6, dating to the later half of the Sixth Dynasty,[27] also serves to show a difference in proportion that becomes evident from the Eleventh Dynasty onward;[28] the limbs of *Ip* are slightly more slender, he is higher-waisted, and his head is distinctly smaller.

[23] For the attitude see Harpur, *Decoration*, pp. 127–28 and 323–24.
[24] The leopard skin is occasionally worn by the tomb owner in representations showing exactly the same attitude. For Old Kingdom examples see Junker, *Gîza* VI, fig. 40; Wreszinski, *Atlas zur altägyptischen Kulturgeschichte* III (Leipzig 1936), pl. 69, and Blackman, *Meir* IV, pl. 14. An example of the Heracleopolitan Period is to be found in Kanawati, *Hawawish* IX, fig. 15.
[25] The leopard skin is still worn by the tomb owner in chapels of the early Middle Kingdom: (Newberry, *Beni Hasan* II, pls. 16, 30; Newberry, *Bersheh* II, pl. 16) and at least as late as the reign of Sesostris I (Blackman, *Meir* II, pl. 16; Davies *Antefoker*, pl. 14).
[26] Discussed by Staehelin, *Untersuchungen zur ägyptischen Tracht*, pp. 75–80. In the Twelfth Dynasty its use was soon extended to other funerary priests (e.g., *MMJ* 9 [1974], 24, fig. 33), and then might be attributed to anyone who was represented in the act of invoking offerings for the deceased: e.g., Cairo CG 20088, 20102, 20103, 20681, 20718.
[27] The example from Meir cited in n. 24 above.

17

The left half of the wall is divided into four registers, in which cattle are being led forward, to be recorded by a pair of scribes. All the men have short hair and a simple kilt. In the uppermost register a herd of bulls, represented by reduplicating only the front of four animals, is led by a man who guides a calf, presumably to induce the others.[29] The recording is done by a scribe who sits on the ground, his writing board seemingly held between his legs, along with a palette from which a small bottle of water is suspended at the end of a string. Using both hands, he displays his records for the owner's inspection. In Old Kingdom examples of such scenes the scribe usually stands in presenting a scroll, but he is similarly seated in at least two cases.[30] The signs in front of him, given their arrangement and orientation, oddly seem to refer to his master, but the context is lost, as is all but an occasional trace of the inscription above the cattle.

The isocephaly of the seated and standing figures produces an odd impression, because it has led the artist to make the heads almost equal in size. This lapse does not occur in the second register, where a man endeavors to lead a herd of donkeys by pushing a foal ahead of them.[31] Here the artist has introduced a humorously realistic note by showing the donkeys to be more or less heedless of the herdsman's efforts. The scribe seated before him is still engaged in writing the record. In the two lowermost registers, neither of which is as well preserved, various desert animals are presented: probably addax, followed by wild cattle and, in the bottom register, an ibex.

[28] As Wm. Stevenson Smith observes in his *History of Egyptian Sculpture and Painting in the Old Kingdom* (Oxford 1949), p. 222, tall, slim figures may be seen as early as the Sixth Dynasty in Upper Egypt: e.g., Davies, *Deir el Gebrâwi* II, frontispiece. Rainer Hanke (*ZÄS* 84 [1959], 117), notes that they became more common, however, with the advent of the Middle Kingdom. This is well exemplified by the representation of *Nb-ḥpt-Rˁ* Mentu-hotep and his retinue at the Shatt er-Rigal: H.E. Winlock, *Rise and Fall of the Middle Kingdom in Thebes* (New York 1947), pl. 12. For an early Twelfth Dynasty example see Davies, *Antefoker*, pl. 14, where the head is slightly smaller than in the present case.

[29] In the Old Kingdom the herd was more usually persuaded by a bunch of fodder, as in Wild, *Ti* III, pls. 167–68, although a calf was used as inducement in scenes where cattle were fording a canal (*ibid.*, II, pls. 114, 124), but for Old Kingdom examples like the present one see W.K. Simpson, *Mastabas of the Western Cemetery* (Boston 1980), fig. 30; *Mastabas of Qar and Idu* (Boston 1976), fig. 19; LD II, 31a. For Twelfth Dynasty examples see Blackman, *Meir* I, pl. 11; II, pl. 7; Newberry, *Beni Hasan* I, pl. 30.

[30] See Peter Der Manuelian's survey of the motif in the forthcoming *Studies in Honor of William Kelly Simpson* (Boston 1996); the seated examples, cited in his nn. 31 and 32, are Paget and Pirie, *Ptah-hetep*, pl. 35, and LD II, pl. 22c.

[31] For Middle Kingdom examples of donkeys induced by a foal, which is carried before them, see Newberry, *op. cit.*, pls. 13, 30, and an earlier one in Vol. II of the same work, pl. 7.

A column of signs at the center describes these activities, and the titles and name of the owner are given in three short lines between this column and his figure: (l)[a] Viewing the accounting of production,[b] the calling to account of [the managers][c] by [the assessors(? *ḏзt*)] on the two banks(?).[d] (2) The Priest of the Pyramid *Swt*,[e] (3) One Who Is Privy to the Secret of the Six Lawcourts, the Overseer of the Army, *Ỉp*.

COMMENTS:

(a) Fig. 7 shows further traces, as seen from the photograph.

(b) For *ʿwy* "production" see my *Egyptian Studies* III, chap. 3, n. 44, concerning Berlin 7779 and another inscription, both of which have an epithet beginning with ⌐⌐.

(c) This restoration is virtually certain; for *ḥsb ḥqз(w)* cf. *LD* II, 64; Mariette, *Mastabas de l'Ancien Empire* (Paris 1889), pp. 145, 246 (the latter also in W.K. Simpson, *Offering Chapel of Kayemnofret* [Boston 1992], pl. F); Wild, *Ti* III, pl. 168; G.T. Martin, *Tomb of Hetepka* (London 1979), pl. 11 (9); Dows Dunham and W.K. Simpson, *Mastaba of Queen Mersyankh III* (Boston 1974), p. 18 and fig. 9; Ahmed M. Moussa and Hartwig Altenmüller, *Tomb of Nefer and Ka-hay* (Mainz 1971), p. 24 and pl. 7.

(d) *Ḥr* is certain, *ỉdbwy* less so; this is more usually a term for Egypt (*Wb.* I, 153 [5]), but here it would presumably refer to holdings on either side of the river.

(e) The sign ♀ is clearly visible near the end of the preceding column, and the traces after it preclude any element that might be interpreted as the first part of the pyramid's name. Furthermore, although the word *nht* "sycamore tree" is evidently divided between one column and another (L14–15), it is unlikely that a title would be split in this manner, and separated by such a distance.

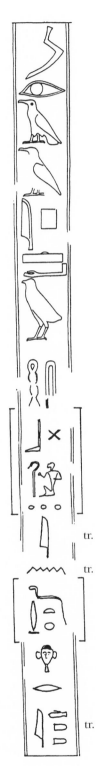

tr.

tr.

tr.

Fig. 7

4. The titles of *Ip*

Ip's TITLES ARE LISTED in the order in which they are mentioned in the foregoing sections:

1.
2.
3.
4.
5.
6.
7.
8.
9.
10.
11.

12.
13.
14.
15.
16.
17.
18.
19.
20.
21.
22.

1. *smr-wꜥty* (L3, 18, R5) "Sole companion." The lowest of the titles of rank, frequent in both the Old and Middle Kingdom: Murray, *Index*, pls. 39–40; Ward, *Index*, no. 1299.

21

2. *iry nfr-ḥꜣt* (L3) "Keeper of the diadem." Ward, *Index*, nos. 521–522. Note that the writing of *iry* conforms to Old Kingdom usage, as opposed to Middle Kingdom 𓀭, 𓁹⊂ or ⌒. Old Kingdom examples of the title are much more numerous: Murray, *Index*, pls. 26–27; Cairo CG 1431, 1569–70 (with 1673, 1702), 1577, 1579, 1756: Junker, *Gîza* X, p. 111; Hassan, *Gîza* I, pl. 30c; II, fig. 86; VI/3, fig. 188; etc.

3. *mr zmit imntt* (L4) "Overseer of the western desert." For normal writings of this title see Ward's *Index*, no. 341; also attested from the Old Kingdom (W.K. Simpson, *Kawab, Khafkhufu I and II* [Boston 1978], figs. 42–44, 46, 49), as is *imy-r zmit* (LD II, 100b; Hassan, *Gîza* VII, fig. 42). The present example confirms Franke's reading of ⊂/𓐍/⊂𓄿 (in Ward's nos. 518a and 540) as a variant of *imy-r* (*GM* 83 [1984], 118). Yet it is certain that the title was still interpreted as two words in Dyn. XII; apart from the evidence given by Gardiner and Edel, summarized in my *Titles*, pp. 44–45, there is the example of Cairo CG 20465, where the deceased says he was praised by the officials of his master, who are designated as 𓏇𓄿𓏤𓂋 *imyw-r.f* "his overseers." The variant must have co-existed with the normal form as an abbreviated version of it. It seems doubtful that there is any connection between this and the occasional writing of *imy-r* as 𓄿, as exemplified by a stela of the Heracleopolitan Period in my *Coptite Nome*, no. 37, p. 94, and even earlier (Dyn. VI) in Mohamed Saleh, *Three Old Kingdom Tombs at Thebes* (Mainz 1977), pp. 12, 17 and fig. 4; Edward Brovarski, *Dissertation*, p. 455, mentions two other examples from Naga ed-Deir, as well as two dating to the Middle Kingdom. *M* did replace *imy-r* at a much later date, however: see Clère in *Hommages à la mémoire de Serge Sauneron* I (Cairo 1979), p. 352 and n. 3.

4. *imy-r pḥw* (L4) "Overseer of marshlands." Not in Ward's *Index*, though it occurs on the Early Middle Kingdom false door of *Ḥꜣ-išt.f* at Saqqara (Porter-Moss, *Bibiliography* III/2, ed. J. Málek [Oxford 1979], p. 615), but well known from the Old Kingdom: Murray, *Index*, pl. 22; Hassan *Gîza* II, fig. 116; Cairo J 15048 (*Urk.* I, 231): Cleveland 64.91 (publication in progress); Cairo 305; G.A. Reisner, *History of the Giza Necropolis* I (Cambridge, Mass., 1942), fig. 257; Epron et al., *Ti* I, pl. 36.; Lloyd et al., *Excavations at Saqqara* II (London 1990), p. 24.

5. *imy-r ḥwt-iḥwt* (L5) "Overseer of the cattle estate." Not in Ward's *Index*, but again well known from the Old Kingdom: Discussed by Karola Zibelius,

Ägyptische Siedlungen nach Texten des Alten Reiches (Wiesbaden 1978), 149–51, with a list of examples, to which add Cairo CG 1552, Cleveland 64.91; and for her latest examples see now Lloyd, *op. cit.,* pp. 7, 24; in her earlier examples this appears to refer to the capital of Lower Egyptian Nome 3, as also in CG 1552, pertaining to an overseer of this province.

6. *ìmy-r šn-tȝ nb* (L5) "Overseer of all vegetation." Ward's single example, *Index,* no. 378 is probably earlier than the Reunification; (see my *Dendera,* p. 91) but the title occurs that late, or even slightly later, in the last case mentioned below. It is adumbrated as ⌒ 𓍜 as early as Dyn. IV in Cairo J 15048 (cited for no. 4 above; Cherpion, *Mastabas,* pp. 108–109, is certainly right in dating it this early), but in the present form is known from the Sixth Dynasty and the Heracleopolitan Period. Brovarski, *Dissertation,* p. 405, cites other examples, including Wild, *Ti* II, pls. 98, 99; see also J. Capart, *Rue de Tombeaux* (Brussels 1907), pl. 73; Firth and Gunn, *Teti Pyramid Cemeteries,* p. 210 (17); Lloyd et al., *op. cit.,* p. 7; J.E. Quibell, *Excavations at Saqqara (1905–06)* (Cairo 1907), pl. 15.

7. *ìmy-[r]…* (L6) "Over[seer of] …."

8. *ìmy-r šḥty-ḥtpwt* (L6) "Overseer of the two fields of offerings." Ward's *Index* gives no examples; Brovarski, *Dissertation,* p. 548, provides evidence he dates to Dyn. IX. Examples from the Old Kingdom include Capart, *loc. cit.* (where *šḥt* is singular); Cairo CG 1619, Lloyd et al., *op. cit.,* p. 24. I doubt the idea expressed in the last publication, that *šḥt* refers to the fen-goddess, for a pair of fen-goddesses seems unlikely. It is more probably to be associated with the "field of offerings," which occurs as the destination of the deceased in scenes of navigation (e.g., Junker, *Gîza* II, fig. 22; III, fig. 29) and in an offering formula (M.A. Murray, *Saqqara Mastabas* I, pl. 18 [= CG 57190]).

9. *ìmy-[r]…* (L7) "Over[seer of]…."

10. *ìmy-r mšꜥ* (L7, B4) "Overseer of the army." Ward, *Index,* nos. 205–15; Fischer, *Titles,* no. 215a; Murray, *Index,* pl. 22. The army might be a group marshalled for non-military operations such as stone-masonry (Ward's no. 212), but the emphasis placed on the title in *Ìp*'s inscriptions suggests that it was indeed military.

11. *ḥtmty-bìty* (L18, R4) "Chancellor of the King of Lower Egypt." A title of rank, higher than *smr wꜥty.* Very frequently attested from the Middle Kingdom: Ward, *Index,* nos. 1472–76, as also earlier: Murray, *Index,* pls. 38–39. For the

reading see my *Egyptian Studies* III, chapter 4, section 3.

12. *smꜣ* (L18) "*smꜣ*-priest." For this title see Grdseloff, *ASAE* 43 (1943), 357–66. His Old Kingdom example from Akhmim, which is written as it is here, may now be found in Naguib Kanawati, *Hawawish* II, fig. 16c, supplementing Vol. I, fig. 4. For Middle Kingdom examples see Ward, *Index,* nos. 1288–93: Fischer, *Titles.,* no. 1288a and p. 80, providing another example where the god in question is not specified.

13. *rḫ nswt* (R2) "One who is known to the King." Well known from both the Middle and Old Kingdom, but omitted in the *Index* of both Ward and Murray, being considered as an epithet, as it may well be. There remains some doubt about its earlier use and meaning, but it clearly meant "one who is known to the King" in the later Old Kingdom; see my *Egyptian Studies* I, p. 8, n. 15.

14. *ỉmy-r___* (R5) "Overseer of ___" During examination of the photograph shown in pl. 3b with T.G.H. James, he thought he could see detail at the bottom suggesting that the questionable sign might be 🜊, as I have redrawn it in fig. 8. I feel very doubtful about this, and also believe the shape of the top is against it; the only example in which the top is remotely similar is the one I have drawn in Karl Kromer, *Nezlet Batran* (Vienna 1991), p. 48. And "overseer of craftsmen" does not accord very well with the rest of the titulary. I have also considered the possibility that the sign might represent the bottom of the oleander that is emblematic of U.E. nomes 20–21, i.e., the Heracleopolitan Nome, which is the "rearward" of the pair. But once again the shape of the upper part of the sign is not quite suitable, for it does not match the lower part of the emblem as shown in title 19. Quite possibly it may represent an offering table, in the title *ỉmy-r ḫꜣwt,* for which see my *Titles,* no. 290*bis,* and a late Old Kingdom example in Firth and Gunn, *Teti Pyramid Cemeteries,* pl. 11 (1). For variations in the hieroglyph representing the table see Hassan, *Gîza* VI/2, pp. 273–75.

Fig. 8

15. [*ỉmy-r*] *st ḫntyw-š* [*pr-ꜥꜣ*] (R10) "[Overseer] of the bureau of tenant land-holders [of the Great House]." Ward, *Index,* has only three clear examples of a title relating to *ḫntyw-š* (all *ỉmy-r ḫntyw-š,* nos. 304, 306). This one is not known from the Middle Kingdom, but is well attested earlier: Murray, *Index,* pl. 20; Junker, *Gîza* VI, p. 17, figs. 82–84; VII, figs. 8, 50; VIII, fig. 27; Hassan, *Saqqara* II, fig. 3; III, figs. 33, 34b. 40–41, Hassan, *Gîza* I, figs. 125, 155; III, fig. 219; Cairo 1548, 1685; etc. This title is evidently superior to no. 17 below, and there

is no basis for restoring *sḏ,* for which there is no evidence, rather than *ỉmy-r;* cf. W. Helck, *Untersuchungen zu den Beamtentiteln* (Glückstadt 1954), p. 107.

16. *smr pr* (R10) "Companion of the House." Not attested in the Middle Kingdom, although Ward cites two valid examples of *smr-pr-ꜥꜣ* from Sinai (*Index,* no. 1301; cf. my notes on his nos. 1300–1302 in *Titles,* pp. 80–81). *Smr-pr* is very well known from the Old Kingdom: Murray, *Index,* pl. 40.

17. *s[ḥḏ] ḫntyw-š [pr-ꜥꜣ]* (R11) "In[spector] of tenant landholders [of the Great House]." Well attested from the Old Kingdom: e.g., Hassan, *Saqqara* II, figs. 4–5; Junker, *Gîza* VI, figs. 32, 93; VII, figs. 5, 108; VIII, figs. 18, 27; IX, fig. 60; Hassan, *Gîza* I, fig. 125; II, fig. 94; III, fig. 221; IX, fig. 24b. Often combined with title 15 above.

18. *ỉmy-st-ꜥ ḫnt-š pr-ꜥꜣ* (R12) "Functionary of tenant landholding of the Great House." Not in Ward's *Index,* and infrequent in Old Kingdom sources; it is discussed in my *Egyptian Studies* III, chap. 3 and n. 79, in connection with Berlin 7779, which has *st-ꜥwy.*

19. *ỉmy-r nꜥrt* (R13) "Overseer of the Oleander (Upper Egyptian Nomes 20–21)." Here the tree lacks the arm that usually extends from it or is superimposed; cf. an Old Kingdom example quoted by Newberry, *ZÄS* 50 (1912), 79, n. 2, and another, from the Sun Temple of Neuserre: Kees, *ZÄS* 81 (1956), 36. Also Norman Davies, *Ptahhetep and Akhethetep* I (London 1900), pl. 10 (178), II (1901), pls. 14, 16, as a variant of the normal form (*ibid.,* and pls. 10–11), for which cf. Moh. Gamal El-Din Mokhtar, *Ihnâsya El-Medina* (Cairo 1983), p. 35, fig. 10. It also lacks the usual specification of *ḫntyt, phyt,* "Upper" and "Lower," but these adjuncts are supplied by a pair of land-signs. The use of *ỉmy-r* is doubtless normal in this northernmost sector of Upper Egypt, rather than *ḥry-tp ꜥꜣ,* which, in the Sixth Dynasty and the Middle Kingdom, was applied to the more independent governors of the Middle Nomes, and those still farther south; cf. *LÄ* II, cols. 410–15. In the reign of *Nb-ḥpt-Rꜥ* Mentuhotep the nome north of *Ỉp*'s was governed by a man who styled himself as *ḫrp m Ḥqꜣ-ꜥnḏy* "director in the Heliopolitan Nome" (Fischer, *Titles,* p. 28, no. 1163a), but this may have been a lesser position, for the preposition "in" suggests that he was not the sole director.

20. *sḏm sḏmt wꜥ* (R13) "Judge of that which one alone judges." Ward, *Index,* nos. 1503, 1275. and cf. 1040; also my *Titles,* p. 87. For the interpretation see *GM* 128 (1992), 69–71, 80.

21. *ḥm-nṯr Swt* (B2) "Priest of the pyramid 'The Places'." This designation of a pyramid, hitherto unknown, is most perplexing since a great many pyramid names, from both the Old and Middle Kingdom, contain the element *swt*; cf. Helck's list in *LÄ* V, cols. 5–6. Among the possibilities are the pyramid cults of Teti and Merykare, at nearby Saqqara, and that of Sesostris I at Lisht, which is even nearer. I doubt, however, that *Ἰp*'s tomb is as late as the last of these. *Ḥm-nṯr* priests are well known from the Old Kingdom: Murray, *Index,* pls. 30–31. Their existence in the Middle Kingdom is attested by the titles of overseers and inspectors of priests: Ward, *Index,* nos. 273, 1327–29, 1331, and my *Titles,* no. 1328a.

22. *ḥry-sštз n ḥwt-wrt 6* (B3) "He who is privy to the secret of the six law-courts." This is known from the Old Kingdom: LD *Ergänzungsband,* pl. 41; and cf. "he who is privy to the judgement (*wḏc mdw*) of the six lawcourts": Oriental Institute, *Mastaba of Mereruka* (Chicago 1938), pl. 212a, which also occurs in Reisner's Giza tomb 2375. Not in Ward, *Index,* but he lists several overseers of the six great lawcourts (no. 248; see also my *Titles,* no. 143a), and his no. 255 mentions an overseer of the six courts in *Ἰṯ-tзwy*.

In sum, only eight of these titles are equally well known from the Old and Middle Kingdom. They include the two titles of rank (1, 11), the honorific no. 13, the courtly title no. 2, the priestly titles *smз* (12) and *ḥm-nṯr* (21), and "overseer of the army" (10), as well as "overseer of the western desert" (3), which may be related to that title and/or the custody of nomes 20–21.

Only one title is distinctly Middle Kingdom (no. 20), and it is related to the judicial title no. 22.

Four of the distinctly Old Kingdom titles are related to the marshes (4), cattle (5), crops (6), and offerings (8), all of which are fairly frequently associated in other titularies, to which reference is made in the preceding notes:

Cleveland 64.71 (4, 5).
Cairo J 15048 (4, 6).
Epron, Wild, *Ti* (4, 5, 6).
Capart, *Rue de Tombeaux,* pl. 73 (6, 8).
Lloyd et al., *Saqqara Tombs* II, p. 7 (5, 6).
Ibid., p. 24 (4, 5, 8).

The other distinctively Old Kingdom titles are likewise interrelated (15, 17, 18), all pertaining to the "tenant farmers," except for the intervening courtly title *smr-pr* (16). They are presented, as expected, in descending order of importance.

The title relating to Upper Egyptian Nomes 20–21 (no. 19) likewise seems to conform to Old Kingdom usage.

The remaining titles are incomplete (7, 9) or problematic (14).

5. The date and situation of *Ip*

THE IMPORTANCE OF DATING THE TOMB lies in the fact that the owner, although buried not far from Atfih, which is mentioned in one of his wife's epithets, and thus presumably a resident of Upper Egyptian Nome 22, was nonetheless assigned the administration of Nomes 20–21, including the capital of the Heracleopolitan rulers. His situation recalls that of the Theban *In-it.f* who was placed in the same region by *Nb-ḥpt-Rˁ* Mentuhotep, apparently to exercise his duties as "overseer of the prison of the great doorway," i.e., of the fortress situated there.[32] *Ip* may similarly have been appointed, perhaps by virtue of his valor as "overseer of the army," to replace the local authority of the vanquished Heracleopolitans. He evidently did not have the high-ranking title of *ḥ3ty-ˁ*, however, as other nomarchs did. Nor is he known to have been nomarch of his own province, although he may possibly have been designated as such in one of the lacunae (e.g., L6).

As might be expected from these circumstances, there are several indications that the decoration of his tomb did, in fact, follow the demise of that regime. It has been shown (Fig. 3) that the offering formula must have applied the epithet *nṯr ˁ3 nb 3bḏw* to the name of Osiris, first attested from the reign of Mentuhotep I, and that the arrangement of signs in this epithet probably entailed a horizontal ⟷, first attested in the 46th year of *Nb-ḥpt-Rˁ*.[33] The title "judge of that which one alone judges" (R13) is first known from a Saqqara false door that is probably slightly later than the Reunification. Further indications of at least this late a date are the use of ⩍ for "overseer" (L4) and the use of *siḥ* instead of *sˁḥ* in the word for "dignitary" (L10). Also, most importantly, the names *Ip*, *Mnḫt* and *Ktt,* all of which are unknown before the Middle Kingdom.

---

[32] MMA 57.95: *JNES* 19 (1960), 258–68. As pointed out in *Artibus Asiae* 22 (1959), 240–52, his stela shows Memphite influence, evidently as a result of his stay in the north.

[33] Schenkel, *Frühmittelägyptische Studien* (Bonn 1962), §4, referring to BM 1203 (*Hieroglyphic Texts* I, pl. 53) and Turin 1447 (Porter-Moss, *Topographical Bibliography* I² [Oxford 1960], p. 331).

As is usual in such cases, it is more difficult to determine precisely how late the chapel may be, but it cannot be much later than the very beginning of the Twelfth Dynasty, as is indicated by the use of ⬭ rather than ⬭ (B2),[34] by 𓊽 rather than 𓊽,[35] and by the complete absence of 𓀀 for the first person singular suffix after nouns, prepositions and verbs. Also note the use of ⬭ in the title *iry ḥ3t-nfr* (L3), instead of the usual Middle Kingdom writing of this as 𓄿 or 𓏏⬭. The older writing of "revered" as *im3ḫw* (R6) rather than *im3ḫy* is less conclusive, especially since 𓄿 appears more frequently.[36] The use of *sk*, rather than *isk*, or *ist*,[37] is again less conclusive.

The iconography of the scenes would suit a somewhat earlier date, although its adherence to Old Kingdom tradition may in part be explained by the nearness of the Memphite cemeteries. The same is generally true of the palaeographic evidence, although the signs 𓄿 , 𓆓 , and ⬭ are more frequently reversed than would be expected before the end of the Old Kingdom,[38] not to speak of 𓏺 and ⬭,[39] and the use of retrograde sequence is more extensive. As might be expected, a stroke (𓏤) is added a little more frequently than in the Old Kingdom, and plural marks are added to titles where they were formerly omitted, although they take the old form ∘∘∘ rather than 𓏼. The sign for "west" (L4) is like Old Kingdom 𓋀, although the stand is missing; in the offering formula (L18) it appears to have the later form 𓋁, which is first exemplified above ground in the Sixth Dynasty.[40] The phraseology (especially the phrases

---

[34] Schenkel, *op. cit.*, §2.

[35] See my *Ancient Egyptian Calligraphy* (New York 1979), p. 24, and *Egyptian Studies* III, chap. 14, end of section 5.

[36] For *im3ḫy* see Schenkel, *op. cit.*, §§16b, 18d; also *Festschrift Elmar Edel* I (Bamberg 1979), 385–87. The writing 𓄿 is rare until the Heracleopolitan Period (Fischer, *Dendera*, p. 131 and n. 578; see also *Egyptian Studies* I, pp. 51–52, where some earlier examples are cited).

[37] Edel, *Altäg. Gramm.*, §852; Gardiner, *Egyptian Grammar*, §§230–31.

[38] The reversal of ⬭ is not uncommon in the Heracleopolitan Period (*JAOS* 76 [1956], 101), but here it is semi-reversed: ⬭ (thus in L3, R5, 13, the first two examples among signs facing right, the third among those facing left). This semi-reversal occurred as early as the Sixth Dynasty at Thebes; see *BiOr* 36 (1979), 32 (g). In the Old Kingdom and down to Dyn. XI, the sign 𓄿 was often subject to semi-reversal (Fischer, *Egyptian Studies* III, chap. 14, section 6), and this may have led to its complete reversal in the present case.

[39] The latter in the name *Ktt* and in compartment 14 of the offering list. These two signs are fairly commonly reversed in Old Kingdom inscriptions, as noted in *Egyptian Studies* II, p. 112.

[40] Ricardo Caminos and H.G. Fischer, *Ancient Egyptian Epigraphy and Palaeography* (New York 1976), p. 33 and n. 21; but the first example cited is actually later than the *Ḥnty-k3* for whom the mastaba was built; see my *Egyptian Studies* III, chap. 1.

in L9–10) and nearly all of the titulary likewise continue Old Kingdom tradition. It is extremely unfortunate, however, that the pyramid-name *Swt*, in title 21, does not provide a more reliable clue.

A more significant indication is perhaps to be found in the fact that the owner holds a jar of ointment in the offering scene,[41] for this motif occurs fairly frequently in representations of the Eleventh Dynasty,[42] but seems to have been abandoned soon after the Reunification.[43] It was revived, albeit much less frequently, on stelae dating to the end of the Twelfth Dynasty and to the Thirteenth,[44] when ointment and incense were emphasized in other ways.[45] It should also be noted that, in the present case, the fastening of the lid is carefully indicated, but, unlike almost all the Eleventh Dynasty examples, the ends of the cord do not project from the seal, any more than they do in the sign ⌣.[46]

[41] See note 8 above. This motif was occasionally replaced by the smelling of a lotus as early as Dyn. VI, although the lotus more usually appeared in the hand of a woman; for details see *JNES* 16 (1957), 224, n. 6.

[42] Louvre C15 (Drioton, *RdE* 1 [1933], pl. 9): Cairo CG 20007; Cairo J 36346; Berlin 1197 (*LD* II, 144s); Turin 1513 (stylistically like the last); Turin 1513; MMA 14.2.6–7 (Winlock, *Rise and Fall of the Middle Kingdom* [New York 1947], pl. 2); Moscow I.1.a.1137 (Svetlana Hodjash and Oleg Berlev, *Egyptian Reliefs and Stelae in the Pushkin Museum* [Leningrad 1982], no. 25); Moscow I.1.a.5603, formerly 4071 (*ibid.,* no. 26); Chatsworth House Collection (H.W. Müller, *MDAIK* 4 [1933], 187).

[43] The only Eleventh Dynasty example definitely known to be later than the Reunification is Louvre C14: Winfried Barta, *Das Selbstzeugnis eines altägyptischen Künstlers* (Berlin 1970), fig. 1 on p. 14, and pl. 1. Another example dating to the late Eleventh Dynasty is probably to be seen in the fragmentary stela of *Id* born of *Hn[wt]*: Sotheby sales catalogue, New York, Nov. 21–22, 1985, no. 118, but it can hardly be any later; note the use of *ms* rather than *ms.n* before the name of the mother (Schenkel, *op. cit.,* §27b) and the phrase "all that my father gave me in town and country," which is very like one that occurs on a somewhat earlier stela from Naga ed-Deir (*Studies... in Honor of Dows Dunham,* [Boston 1981], pp. 65–66 and comment e).

[44] Moscow I.1.a.5349, formerly 4161 (Hodjash and Berlev, *op. cit.,* no. 34); Leiden V103 (P.A.A. Boeser, *Beschrijving van de Egyptische Verzameling* II [The Hague 1909], pl. 13. no. 26), both late Dyn. XII. Later examples: MMA 22.3.308 (W.C. Hayes, *Scepter of Egypt* I [New York 1953], fig. 227); Florence 2579 (Sergio Bosticco, *Le Stele Egiziane* I [Rome 1959], no. 39); Vienna ÄS 96 (Hein and Satzinger, *CAA Wien* 4, p. 4): Vienna ÄS 97 (*ibid.,* p. 8): Vienna ÄS 104 (*ibid.,* p. 17); Boston MFA 72.768 (Leprohon, *CAA Boston,* 2, p. 8); Oslo EM 2383 (Saphinaz-Amal Naguib, *CdE* 55 [1980], 19). It is remarkable that, on the first two stelae in Vienna, a woman holds a jar while a man smells the lotus (and vice versa), as also on the stela in Oslo. This reverses Old Kingdom tradition. In some cases, however, the workmanship is so crude that the lotus and vase are easily confused: e.g., Boeser, *op. cit.,* pl. 23, no. 32.

[45] Cf. my *Egyptian Studies* III, chap. 12 and notes 21–22. Often the jar is simply placed upright near the head of the deceased: e.g., Boeser, *op. cit.,* pls. 9 (no. 16), 22 (no. 26), 24 (no. 34).

[46] All the examples in note 42 above, but not the second one in note 43, nor the second in note 44, but in the late Middle Kingdom such details were readily omitted.

Yet another iconographic link with the Old Kingdom is apparently to be found in the burial chamber, which is discussed in the following section: namely the stalk of papyrus that is held by a female attendant.

In view of all these considerations, I am inclined to think that *ʿIp*'s chapel is no later than the end of the Eleventh Dynasty. It is more difficult to say—given the variability of longevity in ancient times—when he began his career, and whether the king who put him in charge of Upper Egyptian Nomes 20–21 may have been *Nb-ḥpt-Rʿ* Mentuhotep. I think that is possible, however, and even probable. It is, at any rate, most improbable that Amenemhet I, having moved his capital just north of the Heracleopolitan Nome,[47] would have appointed an official of middling rank to govern it. And were *ʿIp* a protégé of this ruler, one might expect him to have made his tomb at Lisht.

If *ʿIp*'s governorship goes as far back as the Reunification, some of his other titles may have been acquired even earlier, by appointment or by inheritance. It may be noted that the titulary of *Dgi*, a vizier of *Nb-ḥpt-Rʿ* Mentuhotep, also shows a number of Old Kingdom titles in his tomb at Thebes, among which are some obvious archaisms.[48] But I doubt that, in the present case, the Old Kingdom titles are mere *iꜣwt ḥrt-nṯr* "offices of the necropolis";[49] for *ʿIp* does not claim the high-ranking title *ḥꜣty-ʿ*, and his biographical statements modestly reflect obedience and submission. It seems particularly unlikely that the three titles referring to the *ḫntyw-š* are simply window dressing. But these possibilities only point up the complexity of the many questions that surround his geographical and chronological situation. His career will certainly be subject to further debate, but, unless additional evidence is forthcoming, it is almost equally certainly destined to remain a tantalizing puzzle.

---

[47] For the location of *Iṯ-tꜣwy* in Lower Egyptian Nome 1 see W. Helck, *Die altägyptischen Gaue* (Wiesbaden 1974), p. 149; also Gomaà, *Besiedlung* II, p. 38.

[48] N. de Garis Davies, *Five Theban Tombs* (London 1913), pls. 32, 34, 38; especially Ward, *Index*, no. 1131, for which see also my *Titles*, p. 74, and no. 1313a (*ibid.*, p. 34); also 1148 (*ibid.*, p. 75), which is elsewhere preceded by *r Py nb* "mouth of every Butite," but here follows *r Nḫn* "mouth of Nekhen." In Ward's nos. 688, 976 and my 638a it is only the end of the title that gives it its Old Kingdom character; these may be archaic retouchings.

[49] For this phrase see Vandier, *Moʿalla* (Cairo 1950), p. 246, where he cites examples from Dendera and Hagarsa; for the latter cf. *Urk.* I, 267 (3–4). The abuse of the title *ḥꜣty-ʿ* was particularly common at Naga ed-Deir during the Heracleopolitan Period, in contrast to Dendera (Fischer, *Dendera*, p. 71).

6. The burial chamber (Pl. 7)

TWO OF THE FOUR WATERCOLOR PAINTINGS that accompanied the facsimiles of *Ip*'s tomb chapel evidently show parts of a burial chamber, for the representations are completely funerary in character, and the background is more somber—brownish rather than nearly white, as in the chapel. And they are of much lesser height, about 45 cm, with a speckled area below them, doubtless imitating granite. It also seems likely that the paintings come from the same wall; in any case they both refer to the wife.[50]

Whereas the white areas in the chapel seem simply to be left unpainted, here, because of the darker background, they had to be added. And instead of blue, a paler greenish blue is used.

At the left the woman is seated on a chair that has bull's legs; her skin is pale yellow and she wears a long white dress as well as a pair of anklets. Before her is the splayed tubular stand for an offering table, beneath which is a solitary vessel. The end of a column of hieroglyphs to the right of this concludes with the words "to thy *kз.*" Still further to the right are the compartments of a long list of offerings, each followed by the figure of a man making offering, but the designations of the offerings do not appear to have been inserted.

Below the seated woman is a register showing a pair of men in the act of slaughtering a steer; one holds a foreleg of the animal straight up in order to cut its throat,[51] while the other extends a bowl to receive the blood. They are flanked by a pair of women bearing offerings, each wearing a long white dress and long lappeted wig; the one on the left holds a bloom and bud of blue lotus in one hand, while raising the other to balance a load on her head. The second carries a fowl in each hand, and balances a tray of fruit on her head. Behind

---

[50] Some photographs were taken of details in the scenes, but they add nothing to what is shown in the color copies.

[51] Cf. E. Naville, *The XIth Dynasty Temple of Deir El-Bahari* III (London 1913), pl. 3; H.E. Winlock, *Excavations at Deir el Bahri 1911–1931* (New York 1942), pl. 8.

her are a group of four men, who perform the offering ritual; the first kneels before a basin mounted on a stand, while the man behind him prepares to pour a libation of natron from a *ḥz*-jar. The third appears to present a leg of beef, which is in itself the most usual of offerings but is unexpected among the ritualists as is its color, which should be red, not white;[52] I think it more likely that the object in his hand is a roll of papyrus. The last officiant makes the gesture of invocation. He has a long wig and wears the distinctive bandoleer of the lector priest. All the men have tight-fitting kilts with the possible exception of the man making a libation, and all but the lector priest are wigless.

At the right end of the wall an inscription at the top begins the offering formula with *ḥtp dì nswt* "an offering that the king gives." Below this are three tables, one of which bears a pair of broad collars, while another evidently bears a mirror. The tallest register, at the bottom, shows the figure of a standing woman, wearing a long, greenish-blue dress, a long lappeted wig and a pair of anklets. In one hand she holds a bloom and bud of the blue lotus, while the other presents a long stalk of what seems to be papyrus, to judge from the thickness of the stem and its shape at the bottom. If this identification is correct, it represents a surprising adherence to Old Kingdom tradition, as exemplified in Fig. 9.[53] After the Old Kingdom this motif was generally replaced by a staff topped by a lotus bud,[54] and that would certainly be expected in the Eleventh Dynasty.[55] Two tables, bearing jars of oil and unguent, are ranged before the woman, one above the other, beyond which the remains of two more tables are visible. Above her there are remnants of a line of inscription that faces rightward, pertaining to the deceased woman; they may be restored as follows: [hieroglyphs] "beloved of her [hus]band, p[raised by him]."

Apart from the examples of *Kȝ(.ì)-m-ꜥnḫ* and *Kȝ(.ì)-ḫr-Ptḥ* at Giza,[56] burial chambers are not known to have contained representations of human beings before the advent of the Eleventh Dynasty, at Memphis itself,[57] and at Kom

---

[52] E.g., Davies, *Deir el Gebrâwi* II, pl. 12; C. Vandersleyen, *Das Alte Ägypten*, pl. XXIV. The ritualists have most recently been discussed by Günther Lapp, *Die Opferformel des Alten Reiches* (Mainz 1986), chapter 16.

[53] From Davies, *op. cit.*, pl. 6; the frontispiece shows this detail in color. Cf. also pls. 10, 19, the latter showing what appears to be a long-handled mirror, of unparalleled size.

[54] *Orientalia* 61 (1992), 144–45.

[55] E.g., the scene at the Shatt er-Rigal, cited above, n. 28.

[56] Junker, *Gîza* IV, pp. 43 ff.; VIII, pp. 116–21.

[57] Christine Lilyquist, *JARCE* 11 (1974), 27–30 and pls. 1–3. They are probably to be dated to the end of the Heracleopolitan Period or Dyn. XI.

Ombo.[58] While such representations are scarcely in evidence on the walls of
Eleventh Dynasty burial chambers at Thebes, they did appear, shortly before
the Reunification, on sarcophagi placed within such chambers.[59] This feature
does not seem to argue for a later dating of *Ip*'s tomb than has previously been
suggested.

Fig. 9

[58] Steffen Wenig, *Staatliche Museen zu Berlin: Forschungen und Berichte* 10 (1968), 71–94.
[59] For Eleventh Dynasty sarcophagi see H.E. Winlock, *op. cit.*, pls. 8, 10; for burial chambers pls. 13, 16.
The only exception, in the case of *Nfrw*, is the row of kneeling figures below items in the offering list.

Addenda

p. 13, n. 12. The scenes of rattling papyrus in the marshes are also discussed by Hartwig Altenmüller in *Kunst des Alten Reiches: Symposium im Deutschen Archäologischen Institut Kairo am 29. und 30. Oktober 1991* (Mainz 1995), pp. 20–27.

p. 24, title 14. In respect to my final suggestion concerning the sign ⎄, Dorothea Arnold has shown me pictures of a fragmentary piece of painted relief which shows a rather similar offering table as well as two footed goblets that look like the table in miniature, one of which is presented to the seated figure of the deceased. The fragment was excavated at Lisht South in 1992, and has been provisionally assigned to the First Intermediate Period on account of its crudeness of style.

In addition, James Allen tells me that the Twelfth Dynasty offering table from Lisht, CG 23053, has ⎄ at the end of the feminine name *Qbˁt*, and not ▽ as shown by Ranke, *PN* I, 333 (24). Its application in this context is obscure, for the meaning of the name is unexplained.

Abbreviations

ASAE	*Annales du Service des Antiquités de l'Egypte*, Cairo
BdE	*Bulletin de l'Institut de l'Egypte*, Cairo
BiOr	*Bibliotheca Orientalis*, Leiden
BM	The British Museum
Brovarski, *Dissertation*	E. Brovarski, *The Inscribed Material of the First Intermediate Period from Naga ed-Dêr.* University of Chicago Ph.D. dissertation, Dec. 1990
CAA	*Corpus Antiquitatum Aegyptiacarum*, Mainz
Cairo CG	Numbers referring to *Catalogue général des antiquités égyptiennes du Musée du Caire:*
CG 1–1294	L. Borchardt, *Statuen und Statuetten*, Berlin 1911–1936
CG 1294–1808	L. Borchardt, *Denkmäler des Alten Reiches* I–II. Berlin 1937–1964
CG 17001–17036	C. Kuentz, *Obélisques.* Cairo 1932
CG 20001–20780	H.O. Lange and H. Schäfer, *Grab- und Denksteine des Mittleren Reichs.* Berlin 1902–1925
Cairo J	Egyptian Museum, Cairo, Journal d'Entree

CdE	*Chronique d'Egypte*, Brussels
Cherpion, *Mastabas*	Nadine Cherpion, *Mastabas et Hypogées d'Ancien Empire*. Brussels 1989
CT	A. de Buck, *The Egyptian Coffin Texts*, 7 vols. Chicago 1935–1961
Davies, *Antefoḳer*	Norman de G. Davies, *The Tomb of Antefoḳer*. London 1920
Davies, *Deir el Gebrâwi*	Norman de G. Davies, *The Rock Tombs of Deir el Gebrâwi* I–II. London 1902
Edel, *Altäg. Gramm.*	Elmar Edel, *Altägyptische Grammatik* I–II. Rome 1955–1964
Epron et al., *Ti*	L. Epron, F. Daumas, G. Goyon, P. Montet, *Tombeau de Ti* I. Cairo 1939
Firth and Gunn, *Teti Pyramid Cemeteries*	C.M. Firth and B. Gunn, *Excavations at Saqqara; Teti Pyramid Cemeteries*, 2 vols. Cairo 1926
Fischer, *Coptite Nome*	H.G. Fischer, *Inscriptions from the Coptite Nome*. Rome 1964
Fischer, *Dendera*	H.G. Fischer, *Dendera in the Third Millennium B.C.* Locust Valley, N.Y. 1968
Fischer, *L'écriture*	H.G. Fischer, *L'écriture et l'art de l'Egypte ancienne*. Paris 1986
Fischer, *Egyptian Studies*	H.G. Fischer, *Egyptian Studies* I: *Varia*. New York 1976. II: *The Orientation of Hieroglyphs*. New York 1977. III; *Varia Nova*. New York (in press)
Fischer, *Titles*	H.G. Fischer, *Egyptian Titles of the Middle Kingdom: A Supplement to Wm. Ward's INDEX*. New York 1985

Gardiner, *Egyptian Grammar*	A.H. Gardiner, *Egyptian Grammar*, 3rd ed. London 1957
GM	*Göttinger Miszellen*, Göttingen
Gomaà, *Besiedlung*	Farouk Gomaà, *Die Besiedlung Ägyptens während des Mittleren Reiches* I: *Oberägypten*, II: *Unterägypten*. Wiesbaden 1986, 1987
Harpur, *Decoration*	Yvonne Harpur, *Decoration in Egyptian Tombs of the Old Kingdom*. London 1987
Hassan, *Gîza*	Selim Hassan, *Excavations at Gîza* I–X. Oxford–Cairo 1932–1960
Hassan, *Saqqara*	Selim Hassan, *Excavations at Saqqara 1937–1938* I–III. Cairo 1975
Janssen, *Trad. Autobiogr.*	J. Janssen. *De Traditioneele Egyptische Autobiografie vóór het Nieuwe Rijk*, I (of 2 vols.) Leiden 1946
JAOS	*Journal of the American Oriental Society.* Baltimore, New Haven
JARCE	*Journal of the American Research Center in Egypt*, Boston, Princeton, New York
Junker, *Gîza*	H. Junker, *Gîza* I–XII. Vienna 1929–1955
Kanawati, *Hawawish*	Naguib Kanawati, *The Rock Tombs of El-Hawawish: The Cemetery of Akhmim* I–IX. Sydney 1980–1989
Kêmi	*Kêmi: Revue de Philologie et d'archéologie égyptiennes et coptes*, Paris

LÄ	*Lexikon der Ägyptologie.* I–VII, edited by W. Helck, E. Otto, W. Westendorf. Wiesbaden 1975–1992
L*D*	C.R. Lepsius, *Denkmäler aus Ägypten und Äthiopien*, Abt. 1–6. Berlin 1849–1859
L*D Ergänzungsband*	C.R. Lepsius, *Denkmäler aus Ägypten und Äthiopien. Ergänzungsband.* Leipzig 1913
MDAIK	*Mitteilungen des Deutschen Archäologischen Instituts Abteilung Kairo*, Wiesbaden, Mainz
MMA	The Metropolitan Museum of Art, New York
MMJ	*Metropolitan Museum Journal*, New York
Murray, *Index*	M.A. Murray, *Index of Names and Titles of the Old Kingdom.* London 1908
Newberry, *Beni Hasan*	P.E. Newberry, *Beni Hasan*, 4 vols. London 1893–1900
Newberry *Bersheh*	P.E. Newberry, *El Bersheh*, 2 vols. London 1895
Paget and Pirie, *Ptah-hetep*	R.F.E. Paget and A.A. Pirie, *The Tomb of Ptah-hetep* (with Quibell, *The Ramesseum*). London 1898
PN	H. Ranke, *Die ägyptischen Personennamen*, 2 vols. Glückstadt 1935, 1952
RdE	*Revue d'Egyptologie*, Paris
Urk. I	Kurt Sethe, *Urkunden des ägyptischen Altertums* I: *Urkunden des Alten Reichs*, 2nd ed. Leipzig 1933

Ward, *Index*	W.A. Ward, *Index of Egyptian Administrative Titles of the Middle Kingdom.* Beirut 1982
Wild, *Ti*	H. Wild, *Le Tombeau de Ti* II–III. Cairo 1953, 1966
Wb.	A. Erman and H. Grapow, *Wörterbuch der ägyptischen Sprache,* 5 vols. Leipzig 1926–1953
WZKM	*Wiener Zeitschrift für die Kunde des Morgenlandes,* Vienna
ZÄS	*Zeitschrift für Ägyptische Sprache und Altertumskunde,* Leipzig, Berlin

PLATES

Pl. 1. Left wall

Pl. 2. Left wall

a

b

c

Pl. 3. Right wall

Pl. 5. Rear wall

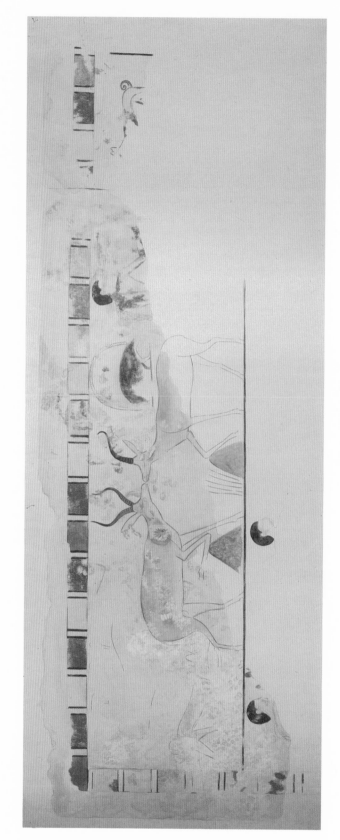

Pl. 6. Right wall

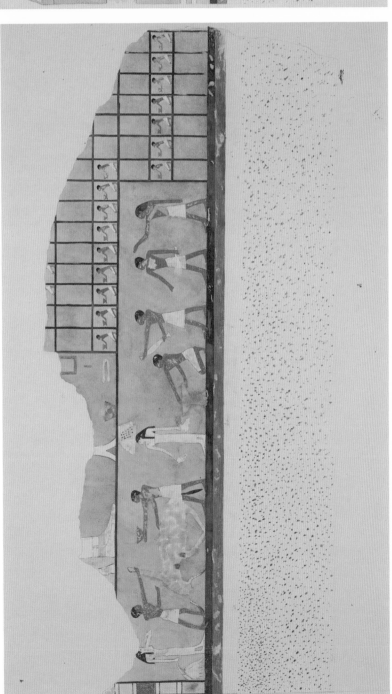

Pl. 7. Wall of wife's burial chamber

Pl. B. Left wall, left end

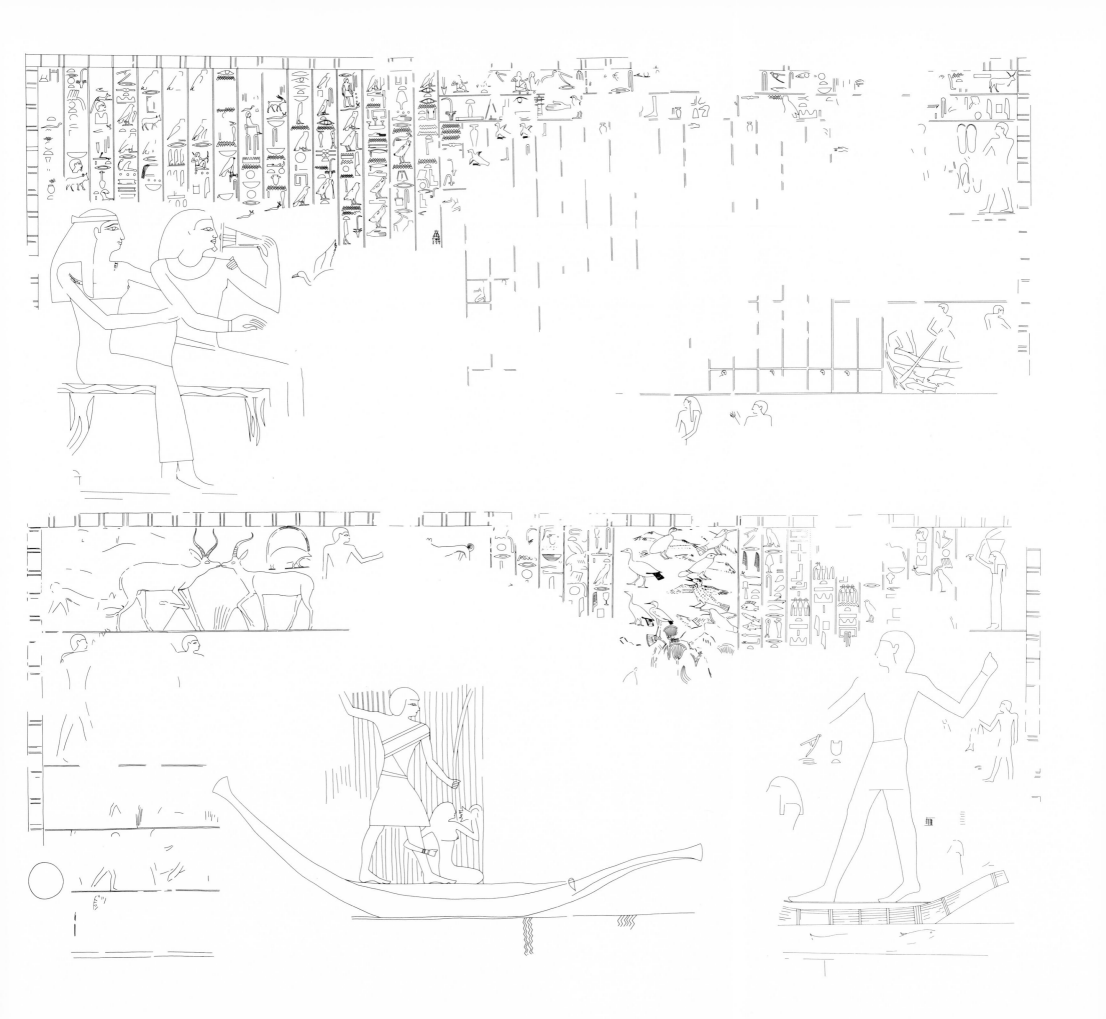

Pl. A. Assembled drawings of left and right walls

Pl. B. Left wall, left end

Pl. B

Pl. C. Left wall, right end

Pl. C

Pl. D. Right wall, left end

Pl. D

Pl. E. Right wall, center

Pl. F. Right wall, right end

Pl. G. Rear wall